FROM SEA to SHINING SEA

# INDIANA

## BETTINA LING

*Consultants*

**MELISSA N. MATUSEVICH, PH.D.**

*Curriculum and Instruction Specialist*
*Blacksburg, Virginia*

**NANCY McGRIFF**

*Library Media Specialist*
*South Central Community Schools*
*Union Mills, Indiana*

**LINDA CORNWELL**

*National Literacy Specialist*
*Paperbacks and Teacher Resources*
*Scholastic Inc.*

**CHILDREN'S PRESS®**

A DIVISION OF SCHOLASTIC INC.

New York · Toronto · London · Auckland · Sydney · Mexico City
New Delhi · Hong Kong · Danbury, Connecticut

Indiana is in the midwestern part of the United States. It is bordered by Michigan, Ohio, Kentucky, Illinois, and Lake Michigan.

The photograph on the front cover shows an Amish carriage and farms near Middlebury.

Project Editor: Meredith DeSousa
Art Director: Marie O'Neill
Photo Researcher: Marybeth Kavanagh
Design: Robin West, Ox and Company, Inc.
Page 6 map and recipe art: Susan Hunt Yule
All other maps: XNR Productions, Inc.

Library of Congress Cataloging-in-Publication Data

Ling, Bettina.
    Indiana / by Bettina Ling.
        v. cm. — (From sea to shining sea)
Includes bibliographical references and index.
Contents: Introducing the Hoosier state—The land of Indiana—Indiana through history—
Governing Indiana—The people and places of Indiana—Indiana almanac—Timeline—
Gallery of famous Hoosiers.
    ISBN 0-516-22387-9
    1. Indiana—Juvenile literature. [1. Indiana.] I. Title. II. Series.
    F526.3 .L56 2003
    977.2—dc21                                        2002001605

CHILDREN'S PRESS and associated logos are trademarks and or registered trademarks of Grolier Publishing Co., Inc. SCHOLASTIC and associated logos are
trademarks and or registered trademarks of Scholastic Inc.
1 2 3 4 5 6 7 8 9 10 R 12 11 10 09 08 07 06 05 04 03

# TABLE of CONTENTS

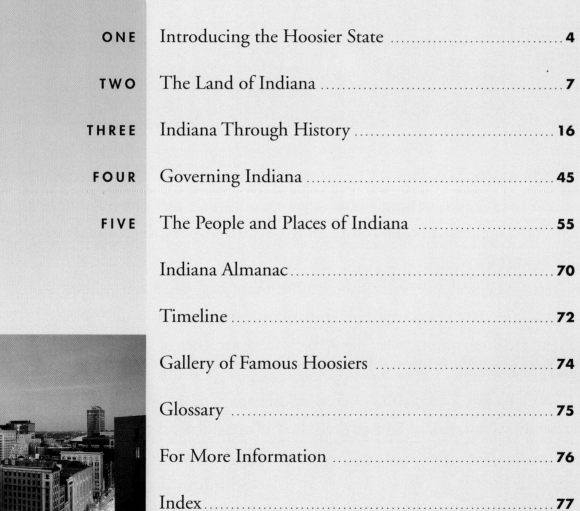

# CHAPTER ONE

# INTRODUCING THE HOOSIER STATE

Indiana is a blend of small communities, rural farms, and big cities.

**I**ndiana's state motto is **"Crossroads of America."** The name refers to the many roadways, waterways, and railways that cross through the state, making it home to one of the best transportation systems in the country.

However, Indiana offers much more than just good transportation routes. Acres of quiet rolling farmland stretch alongside busy cities. There are thick forests, numerous lakes, long stretches of sandy beaches, and small friendly towns hidden away off peaceful country roads.

Indiana has a long and interesting history. The name *Indiana* was created by Congress in 1800, when the Indiana Territory was organized out of the Northwest Territory. It means "the land of the Indians" and refers to the many Native American tribes who lived in the region at that time.

Since then, Indiana has grown to include people of many backgrounds. Together, Indiana's more than 6 million residents are known as Hoosiers, after the state's nickname, the Hoosier State. There have been many ideas about how it got this nickname, though no one knows exactly where it came from.

What comes to mind when you think of the Hoosier State?

- Exciting automobile races at the Indy 500
- Winning basketball teams such as the Indiana Pacers and the Indiana Hoosiers
- Great universities such as Indiana University, Notre Dame, and Purdue
- Vacationers enjoying the Indiana Dunes National Lakeshore
- Barges traveling the Ohio River
- Ancient Native American mounds at the Angel Mound Historic Site
- Amish families riding in horse-drawn buggies

Indiana has many natural wonders and fascinating places. Read on to find out the story of the Hoosier State and why its people and places are so intriguing.

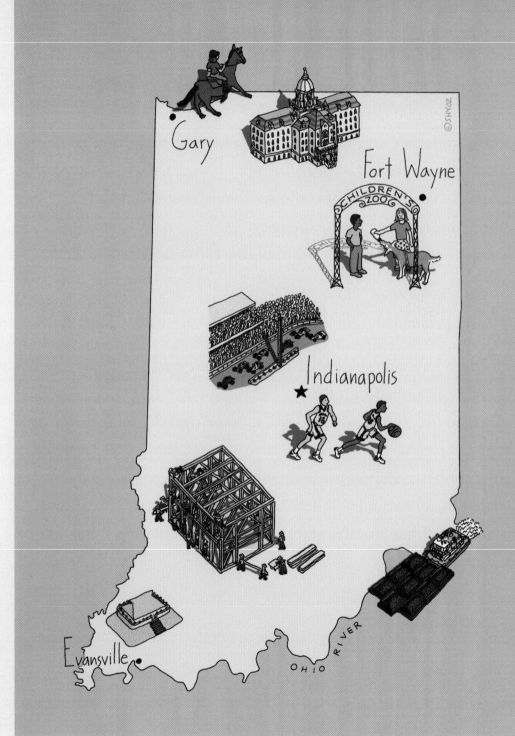

Gary

Fort Wayne

CHILDREN'S ZOO

Indianapolis

Evansville

OHIO RIVER

# CHAPTER TWO

# THE LAND OF INDIANA

**I**ndiana is one of twelve states that make up the midwestern part of the United States (the north central part of America). Indiana is the smallest of the midwestern states, at just over 36,420 square miles (94,327 square kilometers), including 550 square miles (1,424 sq km) of water. It is bordered to the west by Illinois, to the north by Michigan, and to the east by Ohio. The Ohio River forms Indiana's southern border along with Kentucky. Lake Michigan, one of the Great Lakes, touches the northwest corner of the state.

Kayakers make their way down Sugar Creek at Turkey Run State Park.

## GEOGRAPHIC REGIONS

Most of Indiana's landscape was formed by glaciers, or huge sheets of ice, that covered much of the state during a time called the Ice Age, which ended about 10,000 years ago. In some places, the movement of the heavy ice pushed, dragged, and carried rocks and soil across the land, forming low hills of earth and rocks called moraines. In other regions, the huge glaciers flattened the earth and left a deep layer of till—a mixture of sand, clay, gravel, and boulders. Thick piles of till filled many valleys and covered hills.

After the glaciers melted, the area we now call Indiana was left with three distinct natural regions: the Northern Lake and Moraine region, the Till Plains, and the Southern Hills and Lowlands.

### The Northern Lake and Moraine Region

The Northern Lake and Moraine region covers the northern half of the state. Part of this region borders Lake Michigan, the third largest of the five Great Lakes. Along the lakeshore are long stretches of white sand dunes that make up the Indiana Dunes National Lakeshore. This

Indiana Dunes National Lakeshore contains miles of beaches, sand dunes, bogs, and wetlands. Many unique plants can be found in this environment.

national park has more than 14,000 acres (5,666 hectares) of sand dunes and is filled with many kinds of plants and flowers.

South of the sand dunes, the region has low moraine hills and many lakes, both big and small. Several of the state's largest lakes are there, including Bass Lake, which is Indiana's fourth largest natural lake. The region is dotted with marshes that attract birds such as the sandhill crane.

## The Till Plains

The central part of the state is called the Till Plains, named for the till layers of sand, clay, gravel, and rock left by the glaciers. Through the years, the till turned into the rich soil that the region has today. This soil is excellent for growing crops, making the Till Plains the best farming region of the state.

The Till Plains also contains geologic wonders carved out by the strong flow of melting water from the glaciers. The tall canyons and waterfalls at McCormick's Creek and Turkey Run State Park are examples of these glacier formations. Also in this region is the highest point in Indiana, Hoosier Hill. It is 1,257 feet (383 meters) above sea level.

Indiana's rich soil is ideal for farming.

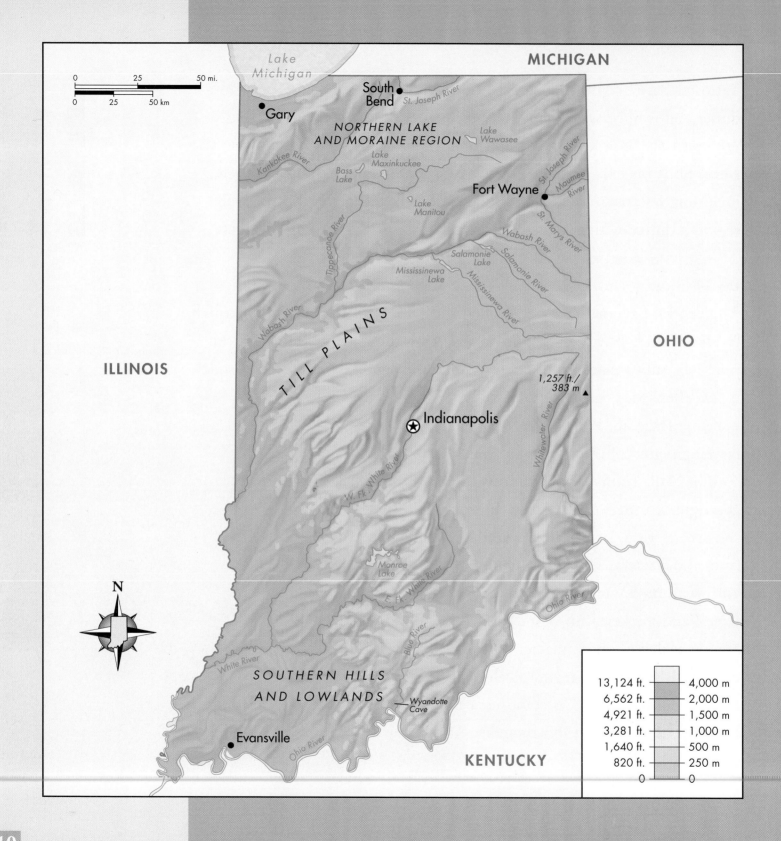

Lake Michigan

MICHIGAN

South Bend

St. Joseph River

Gary

NORTHERN LAKE
AND MORAINE REGION

Lake Wawasee

Kankakee River

Lake Maxinkuckee

Bass Lake

Lake Manitou

Fort Wayne

St. Joseph River

Maumee River

St. Marys River

Wabash River

Tippecanoe River

Salamonie Lake

Salamonie River

Mississinewa Lake

Mississinewa River

Wabash River

T I L L   P L A I N S

ILLINOIS

OHIO

1,257 ft./
383 m

Whitewater River

Indianapolis

W. Fk. White River

Monroe Lake

E. Fk. White River

Ohio River

White River

Blue River

SOUTHERN HILLS
AND LOWLANDS

Wyandotte Cave

Evansville

Ohio River

KENTUCKY

N

0        25        50 mi.

0        25        50 km

| 13,124 ft. | 4,000 m |
| 6,562 ft. | 2,000 m |
| 4,921 ft. | 1,500 m |
| 3,281 ft. | 1,000 m |
| 1,640 ft. | 500 m |
| 820 ft. | 250 m |
| 0 | 0 |

## The Southern Hills and Lowlands

The southern region, known as the Southern Hills and Lowlands, is the only section of the state that was not covered by glaciers. As a result, it has more hills than any other place in Indiana. There are also huge forests and many valleys, steep bluffs, natural bridges, and waterfalls. The rugged bluffs along the Ohio River have great views. Indiana's lowest point, 320 feet (98 m) above sea level, is in Posey County, where the Wabash River flows into the Ohio River.

The southwestern part of this region provides most of Indiana's coal and oil. The southern area also contains large amounts of a rock called Salem limestone. It is the official stone of Indiana. Much of this stone is mined for use in making buildings and other structures.

This region has a number of underground streams. Over time, water from the streams washed out huge hollows (holes) in sections of limestone hills, leaving many underground caves. Two of Indiana's most famous caverns are Wyandotte and Marengo caves. Wyandotte Cave is one of the largest caves in North America. It contains Monument Mountain, an underground mountain that is more than 135 feet (41 m) high.

**FIND OUT MORE**

Limestone is a hard rock made from coral and the remains of shells of marine animals. Shells contain a mineral called calcium, which is also found in the human body. Humans need calcium for strong teeth and bones. What are the names of some other minerals, and what are they used for?

Wyandotte Cave may have been mined by Indiana's early people.

Along with caves, southern Indiana is filled with large forests. The 197,000-acre (79,723-ha) Hoosier National Forest offers endless views of hills and steep ridges, lakes and streams, and hickory, oak, maple, beech, pine, and cedar trees. The region also contains Clifty Falls, the state's highest waterfall. It plunges 100 feet (30 m)—as high as a ten-story building!

Indiana's forests are home to many birds, including yellow-winged sparrows, prairie larks, orioles, swallows, wrens, quail, pheasants, wild turkeys, and cardinals, the state bird. The forests also have deer, muskrats, opossums, rabbits, raccoons, skunks, squirrels, and wood-chucks. Bass, catfish, pickerel, pike, and salmon swim in the lakes and streams.

## RIVERS AND LAKES

The Wabash River is Indiana's longest river, at 512 miles (824 km) long. It flows west across north central Indiana and then turns south to form a long section of the Indiana-Illinois border, emptying into the Ohio River. The Wabash and two of its major branches, or tributaries, the White and Tippecanoe rivers, drain about two-thirds of the state.

The St. Joseph River joins St. Marys River at Fort Wayne to form the Maumee River, which then flows into Lake Erie. Other rivers in Indiana include the Eel, Mississinewa, Salamonie, Kankakee, Whitewater, and Blue. The state's southern boundary runs along the north bank of the Ohio River, but no part of the river flows through the state.

Indiana has about 1,000 natural lakes. Lake Wawasee in the north-eastern part of the state is the largest of Indiana's natural lakes. It covers 4.6 square miles (12 sq km). Other large lakes include Manitou, Maxinkuckee, and Turkey. Some of the largest lakes in the state are man-made. These lakes, called reservoirs, include Mississinewa, Salamonie, and Monroe.

The Wabash River meanders past farmland and small communities in north central Indiana.

Indiana has a humid (wet) climate, with cool winters and warm summers. The average January temperature ranges from 27° Fahrenheit (–3° Celsius) in northern Indiana to 34° F (1° C) in the south. In July, the temperature averages 75° F (24° C) in the north and 77° F (25° C) in the south.

Geographical differences within Indiana affect the climate in small areas of the state. For instance, the relatively warm waters of Lake Michigan cause the surrounding land area to be warmer in the winter and cooler in the summer than places farther inland. Also, the many

Lake Michigan warms the air, protecting northwestern Indiana from very cold weather.

hills, valleys, and forests of southern Indiana can cause temperatures there to vary slightly within short distances.

Rainfall averages 36 inches (91 centimeters) per year in northern Indiana and 43 inches (109 cm) in the south. Dry periods and floods occur occasionally in the south. In northern Indiana, hailstorms (storms with ice and snow pellets) are common, but they occur only occasionally in the south during summer.

In winter, heavy snowfalls are common in the north. Snowfall ranges from more than 40 inches (102 cm) per year in the northern section to about 10 inches (25 cm) per year in the south. Much of the snow in northwestern Indiana is caused by moist air crossing Lake Michigan and turning into snow over land.

Indiana also has its share of tornadoes—violent whirling winds that move at great speeds across land. Tornadoes usually occur in March and April. A series of tornadoes touched down in the upper Midwest and Great Lakes regions on April 11, 1965. Eleven tornadoes struck twenty counties in Indiana, killing 137 people and causing $30 million of property damage. Called the Palm Sunday Outbreak, it was one of the worst tornado outbreaks ever to strike the area.

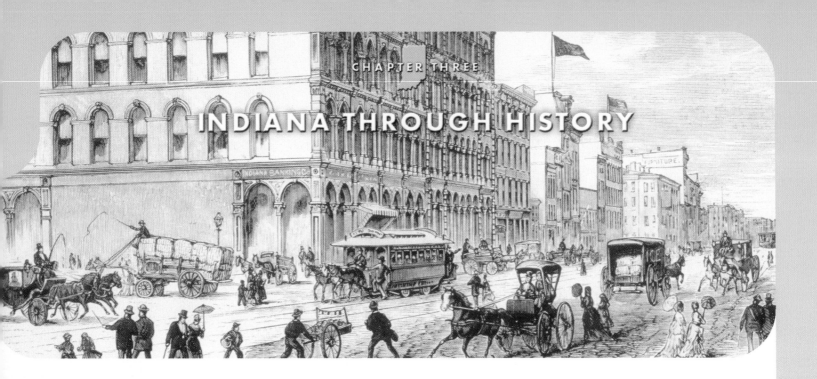

# CHAPTER THREE

# INDIANA THROUGH HISTORY

This drawing shows a view of Washington Street in Indianapolis during the 1870s.

**The first people to live in what is now Indiana** were prehistoric Native Americans called Paleo-Indians. These people came from Canada about 10,000 to 12,000 years ago. They were nomads who moved from place to place hunting large animals such as giant buffalo and woolly mammoth.

By 4000 B.C., descendants of the hunter culture started gathering wild plants, roots, and seeds for food. Instead of moving around like their ancestors, they led a more settled way of life. Some lived near rivers, where they caught fish and shellfish. They made spears and other tools out of stones. These people were known as the Archaic people. They lived in present-day Indiana from about 6,000 to 2,500 years ago.

By 500 B.C., the descendants of the Archaic people were planting crops and trading for goods. These were the Woodland people. This group was the first to make clay pots. Before this culture, animal skins and baskets woven from plants were used as containers.

The Woodland people were made up of different Native American tribes. The Adena and Hopewell were two Woodland tribes who lived in Indiana. They were also known as Mound Builders because they built large earthen mounds. These mounds were created for various reasons, such as for burials or as gathering places for religious ceremonies. Many earthen mounds can still be seen in Indiana today.

By the end of the Woodland period, about A.D. 1000, people were planting corn for food and using bows and arrows instead of spears. Out of the Woodland culture emerged the Mississippian culture. This group of Native Americans, who lived in the region from A.D. 1000 to about 1450, had become quite advanced. They grew crops of corn, beans, and squash. These foods were a big part of their diet. They lived in large villages in the summer, when they would farm and

## EXTRA! EXTRA!

Mounds State Park in Anderson features ten mounds built by the Adena and Hopewell people. The largest, called Great Mound, is believed to have been constructed around 160 B.C. Angel Mounds State Memorial near Evansville has mounds from the Mississippian culture. The largest mound held more than a million objects, such as stone and copper tools, freshwater pearls, clay figures, and shark and bear teeth.

Indiana's earliest residents made homes from bent saplings covered with reed mats.

fish. During the winter, the people broke up into smaller groups and lived in hunting camps as they moved from place to place hunting for meat. The Mississippian culture also built earth mounds for use as temple bases and burial grounds.

During the next few hundred years, other Native American groups lived in Indiana at one time or another. By the late 1600s, the major Native American groups living in the area were the Delaware, the Miami, and the Potawatomi, as well as the Piankashaw, the Shawnee, and the Wea. The largest was the Miami tribe, whose members came from Wisconsin and Illinois.

The Miami still lived much like their ancestors from the Mississippian culture. They lived in wigwams (round-shaped homes made from bent young trees and bark) or longhouses (long, rectangular houses also made from bent young trees and covered with bark or rush mats). Larger, separate structures were used for meetings and ceremonies.

The Miami decorated the animal skins they wore for clothing with bright beads, shells, and paint made from plant materials. Both Miami men and women used a form of tattooing to decorate the skin.

## ARRIVAL OF THE EUROPEANS

The first Europeans entered present-day Indiana in 1679. A Frenchman named René-Robert Cavelier, Sieur de La Salle, led a group of French-Canadian explorers through the Indiana region. They traveled on the St. Joseph and Kankakee rivers to the Mississippi River—a perfect route from Canada to Louisiana, another French territory. La Salle returned to Canada after his exploration of the Mississippi, but he came back to the Indiana region late in 1680 and explored much of the northern area.

The Indiana region had many forests filled with animals, such as beavers and minks, whose skins were valuable to the Europeans. The Native Americans were skilled at hunting and trapping, so French fur trappers came to the region and traded beads, blankets, knives, and whiskey in exchange for animal furs. By 1710, the French were carrying on an active fur trade with the Native Americans.

The British were also involved in the fur trade. To expand their trading territory, they decided to move into the Indiana region. The French had to compete with British traders who tried to convince Native Americans to trade only with them. During the next few years, the French built fur trading posts in the region. To protect their route to the Mississippi, the French built Fort Miami (present-day Fort Wayne) in 1715, Fort Ouiatenon (near what is now Lafayette) in 1717, and Fort Vincennes.

French settlers and missionaries joined the fur traders. The settlers were looking for new land to farm. The missionaries were priests who wanted to teach their Christian beliefs to Native Americans. At

Sieur de La Salle was the first European to explore the land we now call Indiana.

Missionaries preached their religious faith to traders and Native Americans.

Vincennes, missionaries founded Indiana's first permanent European settlement in 1732.

The struggle to gain control of the fur trade led to fighting between the French and the British over the Indiana region and other territories in North America. These fights started the French and Indian War (1754–1763). Some Native Americans, such as the Miami, sided with the French; others allied with the British. Great Britain won the war, and gained control of all the land east of the Mississippi River, including present-day Indiana.

Within a few months, the Native Americans were challenging British rule. Before Europeans arrived, Native Americans lived a simple way of life and moved freely about the land. Although many tribes in the Midwest welcomed the early settlers, the Europeans brought new ways and customs with them that were very different from those of Native Americans. Eventually, Native American lands were taken over by fur traders and settlers, who continually wanted more land.

Many Native Americans began to resent the Europeans, and they joined together to try to drive the British out of the Midwest. In 1763 Pontiac's War (named for an Ottawa tribal chief) broke out. The Ottawa, from the Michigan region, were the leaders of the fight. The

Native Americans were defeated, but not before two of Indiana's major forts, Ouiatenon and Miami, were destroyed by the British.

Worried that the Native Americans would continue to fight, the British tried to make peace with them. They drew up the Proclamation of 1763, a law that said Europeans could not settle on any Native American land in the region. Most settlers, however, ignored the law and settled wherever they pleased.

## INDEPENDENCE

During this time the British controlled colonies, or settlements, along the Atlantic Coast. After many years of living under British rule, the colonists decided it was time to form their own, independent country. They rebelled against Britain, which led to the American Revolution (1775–1783).

The American Revolution was mainly fought between colonists and the British in the East. The only battle in Indiana occurred in 1779, when Virginia troops under military leader George Rogers Clark came into Indiana and Illinois to capture Britain's northwestern territories. Clark's troops defeated the British at Fort

George Rogers Clark led a small group of volunteers across the Wabash River in an effort to save Vincennes from the British.

Vincennes, and that victory helped give the Americans control over the Northwest.

Four years after the battle in Indiana, the colonists won the war. They formed a new, independent nation called the United States. A formal agreement known as the Treaty of Paris (1783) gave the United States all of Britain's territory east of the Mississippi, north to Canada, and south to the border of present-day Florida. The United States now controlled the Indiana region. In 1787, the United States government passed a law known as the Northwest Ordinance. This law created the Northwest Territory, organizing a large area of the Midwest, including Indiana, into one territory.

With its wide-open spaces and fertile soil, the new territory held great promise. New settlers from the eastern and southern parts of the United States came to the Indiana and Ohio regions. The new settlers took over many areas of Native American lands. This made the Native Americans very angry.

The Miami tribe, led by Chief Little Turtle, organized a group that included the Wyandot, Delaware, Shawnee, Ottawa, Miami, Chippewa, Potawatomi, Wea, Kickapoo, Eel River, Piankashaw, and Kaskaskia tribes. Together they fought the settlers in Indiana and Ohio. The United States government sent troops to help the settlers, and Little Turtle's War (1790–1794) began. In 1794, General Anthony Wayne defeated the tribes in the Battle of Fallen Timbers, along the Maumee River. Overpowered by the government army, Native Americans had no choice but to surrender.

As a result, Native Americans gave up most of their lands in Ohio and southeastern Indiana. Some areas in northern and western Indiana and Ohio were "reserved," or set aside for Native Americans. These areas were called reservations. The government promised that these lands would not be invaded by settlers.

## BROKEN PROMISES

Congress (the lawmaking body of the United States government) created the Indiana Territory in 1800. This huge new territory included the present-day states of Indiana, Illinois, and Wisconsin, and parts of Michigan and Minnesota. Vincennes was made capital of the territory. General William Henry Harrison was appointed the first territorial governor. The Indiana Territory eventually became smaller when Michigan Territory was split off in 1805 and Illinois Territory in 1809.

During the next few years, Governor Harrison made more land agreements with Native American groups in Indiana. Native Americans sold their lands in southern Indiana to the United States government. The new land agreements allowed them to keep certain areas in the northern and central parts of the state, saying that no

As the first territorial governor, William Henry Harrison made his home in Vincennes.

European settlers would be allowed on the lands. However, these promises were not kept.

Many Native Americans knew that the agreements were unfair. Two Native American brothers, Tenskwatawa (commonly referred to as the Prophet) and Tecumseh, convinced the Wyandot, Potawatomi, and Delaware tribes to band together and fight to take back their lands.

To avoid another war, Governor Harrison was ordered to destroy Tecumseh's headquarters at Prophetstown, near present-day Lafayette. In 1811, Harrison and his army traveled there while Tecumseh was away. The army surprised Tenskwatawa and the other Native Americans, killing many of them and destroying the village in the Battle of Tippecanoe.

Native Americans suffered a terrible defeat at the Battle of Tippecanoe.

During the next ten years, settlers from the eastern and southern parts of the United States and from Europe came to the Indiana Territory, along with more soldiers to protect them. More tribes in Indiana were forced to give up their land and were pushed onto smaller areas in the central, northern, and western parts of the Indiana Territory. Some tribes, such as the Shawnee, left the region, moving to western territories.

The new settlers were mainly farmers. Farm life was difficult. After obtaining land, a farmer and his family needed to clear the land to make space for a cabin and crops. Then, the farmer could build a shelter and plant the first crops.

There was always a chance that plants would not grow. Crops shared the ground with tall weeds and grass. Often, there was either too much rain or not enough. Sometimes, insects or other animals ate the young plants. One farmer's wife described the problems by saying, "We have at last got our corn planted and it comes up well, but pigeons, crows, moles, and cut worms are trying to destroy all."

Still, Indiana had rich soil, and farming was considered the best way to make a living. Some settlers set up businesses such as general stores. Others opened small factories where people made cloth or tools. Still others owned mills where grains were ground up for flour or wood was

In the early 1800s, much of Indiana was wilderness that had to be cleared for settlement.

**EXTRA! EXTRA!**

In 1816, seven-year-old Abraham Lincoln and his family moved from Kentucky to southern Indiana. They settled near present-day Gentryville, and built a cabin by Little Pigeon Creek. Abe spent his boyhood and teenage years growing up in the Hoosier State. He left at the age of 21 when his family moved to Illinois. In 1861, Abraham Lincoln was elected the sixteenth president of the United States.

cut into boards for building. Villages and towns were settled as the pioneers established their homes and businesses.

## EARLY STATEHOOD

Corydon became the new capital of the Indiana Territory in 1813. In December 1815, the territorial legislature met at Corydon to draw up a petition, or written request, for statehood. The petition was approved by Congress, and on December 11, 1816, Indiana joined the Union as the nineteenth state. Its population totaled more than 60,000. Jonathan Jennings was elected the first governor.

At the time of statehood, most settlers lived in the Ohio and Wabash river valleys in the south. Native Americans still owned most of the land in the central and northern areas. However, the United States government wanted that land, and in 1818, it forced the Potawatomi, Wea, Delaware, and Miami tribes to give up their land in the middle of Indiana. This "purchase" was called the New Purchase. The Native Americans received payment in goods and land grants, none of which were worth very much.

Treaties in 1834, 1838, and 1840 completed the efforts of the United States government to remove the Native American population from Indiana. The Potawatomi were gone from their Indiana lands by 1846. Most of the Miami had moved west of the Mississippi River, as well. By 1846, Indiana was almost completely cleared of the Native Americans who had lived there.

After the Native Americans were forced out, more land was open for pioneers. In 1824, the state government made the town of Indianapolis the new capital and moved there in 1825. Because it was in the center of the state, the town had a better location than Corydon for the government.

By the late 1830s, farming in central and northern Indiana had developed into a big operation. During this time, farm tools and machinery, such as plows, were improved. This made farming easier and helped farmers to increase their harvest. Farmers made bigger profits when they grew only one or two important crops, such as corn and wheat, or raised livestock. By 1860, northern and central Indiana were so productive that Indiana had become one of the leading states in the production of corn, wheat, and livestock.

## THE MACHINE AGE

In the mid 1800s, big changes came to Indiana. Until the early 1800s, products such as tools, clothes, and farm machinery were made by hand. As people discovered how to turn natural resources such as coal, oil, and natural gas into fuel, they began to use the fuel to power machinery. Machines could make products faster and easier. Factories using machinery began to be built all over the United States and the world.

Large areas of coal were discovered in southwestern Indiana during the early 1800s. Mining operations to dig the coal out of the ground were begun near Princeton in 1830. As more factories were built, the demand for coal quickly increased, and the number of mines grew rapidly in the late 1800s and early 1900s.

Indiana was a leader during the Industrial Revolution. Factories were built in many parts of the state.

The new factories produced farm machinery, clothes, and tools, and made it possible to package meat and pork to ship to the eastern states for sale. As farming increased and factories produced more goods, better transportation was needed to move products from one place to another.

Until about 1830, most of the state's farm produce was sent by boat down the Wabash and Ohio rivers to New Orleans. In 1832, Indiana began building better roads, railroads, and canals (channels that connect two bodies of water). The National Road, which began in Maryland, was extended into Ohio, Indiana, and Illinois. Work also started on the Wabash and Erie Canal to connect Lake Erie with the Wabash River. When the canal was completed in 1853, it provided an

## FIND OUT MORE

The early 1800s are part of a time period that is often referred to as the First Industrial Revolution. The word *revolution* means to change completely. The Industrial Revolution refers to a new way of manufacturing that changed businesses not only in Indiana but all over the world. How did the change from hand-made to machine-made goods have an effect on people and businesses?

In 1830, the word *Hoosier* first appeared in a poem called "The Hoosier's Nest." The poem was written by an Indiana man named John Finley. It was widely copied throughout the country. From that time on, Indiana was called the Hoosier State, and its residents were known as Hoosiers. There are some interesting theories about where the name Hoosier comes from. It may be:

- An early settlers' response to a knock on the door—"Who's yere?"
- From *hushers*, the name for Indiana rivermen who were good at hushing people who did not agree with them.
- A Kentucky contractor named Samuel Hoosier, whose Indiana workers became known as Hoosier's men.
- From *hoosa*, an Indian word for corn. (Men taking corn from Indiana to New Orleans were called hoosa men.)
- The response "Whose ear?" which is what a visitor to an Indiana bar would say when he arrived after a fight and found an ear on the floor. (Pioneer men had some mean fighting habits—like biting off ears and noses!)
- From an Old English word, *hoozer*, meaning "high" or "hill."

easier water route to move goods to the East Coast and then on to Europe.

The first major railroad line in Indiana ran between Indianapolis and Madison, and was opened in 1847. More railroads were soon added. By the end of the 1800s, railroads had begun to replace boats and waterways as the main form of transportation between Indiana and the eastern states.

Railroads opened up new markets for Indiana products all over the country.

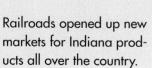

## SLAVERY AND THE CIVIL WAR

As Indiana grew and changed, so did the rest of the United States. People settled in new areas of the country, and various parts of the nation had different ways of living and working. The northern and southern states, for instance, held different views about many issues, including slavery.

In the South, many people used African-Americans to work on large farms called plantations. The African-Americans were called slaves because they were owned by the people they worked for. They had no freedom and suffered cruel punishments for disobeying orders. Slaves were not allowed to read or write. The southern states were known as slave states.

The northern states were known as free states, where it was illegal to own slaves. Northerners worked on farms or in factories or mills and were paid for their work. Many people in the North felt that slavery was wrong.

Slavery was against the law in Indiana. In fact, many Hoosiers spoke out against slavery, and some helped slaves to escape through the Underground Railroad. This was not a train but a chain of people who helped slaves escape from the South into free states or Canada. A religious group in Indiana known as the Society of Friends, or Quakers, was active in the Underground Railroad. The home of Levi and Catharine Coffin, two Indiana Quakers in Newport (today's Fountain City), was a famous stop on the Underground Railroad. They helped more than 2,000 slaves reach safety.

For more than twenty years, Levi Coffin hid slaves in his Indiana home, helping them get to safety. Later, he helped another 1,300 slaves from his home in Cincinnati, Ohio.

## FIND OUT MORE

One of the many slaves who hid in the Coffin home was named Eliza. Eliza's story was told by author Harriet Beecher Stowe in a famous book about slavery, *Uncle Tom's Cabin* (1852). This book helped convince many people that slavery was wrong. What other books tell stories about slavery or the Underground Railroad?

Although most Hoosiers were against slavery, they weren't welcoming to African-Americans. Many Hoosiers worried that free African-Americans would come to Indiana and compete for their jobs and land. To address their fears, the Indiana government put a clause in the state constitution of 1851 that prevented African-Americans from settling in the state. Those who already lived there were allowed to stay but had few rights. They were not allowed to vote or hold public office. They often had trouble finding work or buying land to farm.

Meanwhile, the disagreements between the northern and southern states grew stronger, and in 1861 the southern states seceded, or withdrew, from the United States. They formed a new nation called the Confederate States of America. That same year, Confederate forces opened fire on a Union fort; this was the start of the Civil War (1861–1865).

Although Hoosiers had mixed feelings about slavery, Indiana decided to support the Union. The president of the United States at that time was Abraham Lincoln, who had spent part of his childhood in Indiana. Many Indiana citizens considered him a fellow Hoosier who should be supported. The state contributed 200,000 troops to the Union side. Some Indiana citizens supported the Confederates, however.

The only fighting in Indiana took place in the towns of Corydon, Salem, Dupont, and Versailles in 1863. General John Hunt Morgan led his Confederate cavalrymen, called Morgan's Raiders, across the Ohio River from Kentucky. They attacked the four towns, looting and destroying property, then rode across eastern Indiana into Ohio, where

Morgan's Raiders robbed farmhouses as they passed through Indiana, Kentucky, and Ohio.

Union troops finally stopped them. The North won the Civil War in 1865, and the southern states rejoined the Union.

## THE MANUFACTURING BOOM

After the Civil War, the United States passed laws that gave African-Americans the same rights as other citizens. The Indiana law that prevented African-Americans from settling in the state was declared illegal. African-Americans in Indiana gained the right to vote and to hold office.

The war also had an effect on the state's farmers and businesses. Before the war, farming was the main business for most

## FAMOUS FIRSTS

- The first professional baseball game was played in Fort Wayne in 1871.
- Sylvanus F. Bower invented the gasoline pump in Fort Wayne in 1885.
- The country's first long-distance automobile race on a track took place at the Indianapolis Motor Speedway in 1911.
- The first diesel-powered tractor was made in Columbus in 1930.
- The world's first theme park, Santa Claus Land, opened in Santa Claus in 1946.
- The first transistor radio was manufactured in Indianapolis in 1954.

people in the United States. After the war, the prices for farm products decreased, and the costs to ship the products got higher. Many farmers had borrowed money from the bank to buy machinery and land, leaving them with big debts to pay and not enough money to pay them.

In contrast, manufacturing was doing well. The new factories were productive and goods were cheaper to produce. Manufacturing replaced farming as the biggest industry in the United States. In Indiana, meat-packing and machine factories developed in the northern and central areas of the state. Musical instruments, clothing, glassware, furniture, and toys were produced in city factories. Many farmers gave up farming and looked for work in the factories.

In 1886, natural gas was discovered near Portland, in the east-central region. In 1889, oil was found in Indiana's southwestern region. Like coal, these natural resources could be used for fuel to power engines and machines in factories. Natural gas and oil are mined by pumping them out of the ground. Then they need to be refined, or cleaned, before they are used. Mining and refining operations offered many new jobs.

The discovery of natural gas and oil brought businesses to Indiana from other states. These businesses wanted to be near fuel sources. In 1889, the Standard Oil Company built one of the world's largest oil refineries in the village of Whiting, on Lake Michigan. The automobile industry started in Indiana in 1894 with the invention of the nation's second successful gasoline-powered automobile, the Haynes Pioneer, in Kokomo. Soon, automobile manufacturing plants dotted the state.

Other manufacturing businesses had already started in the state. In 1876, a chemist named Colonel Eli Lilly opened the Lilly Pharmaceutical Company in Indianapolis. It would grow to become one of the biggest drug companies in the world.

The plentiful factory jobs brought people from European countries such as Germany, Scotland, and Norway to the state.

The United Mine-Workers of America was an important force in gaining workers' rights.

Although there were many jobs available, the work was difficult. Employees were often not paid enough, and they worked under dangerous conditions. Factory workers and miners joined together to demand better wages and working conditions. These organized labor groups had some effect. By 1897, many labor laws had been passed in Indiana to help protect workers and miners.

Workers and miners weren't the only people making changes in Indiana. Many Indiana women had joined the women's rights movement. This was a nationwide rallying of women to fight for equal rights. At the time, American women did not have the same rights as men. In most states, they could not vote, control their money, or own property. Women wanted these rights and banded together to fight for them.

## WHO'S WHO IN INDIANA?

**May Wright Sewall (1844–1920)** was one of the leaders in the women's movement. Born in Milwaukee, Wisconsin, she moved to Indianapolis with her husband in 1872. She helped found the Girls' Classical School, one of the three leading girls' schools in Indianapolis. She also became widely known for her efforts in the women's rights movement in the United States and around the world.

## WHO'S WHO IN INDIANA?

**Benjamin Harrison (1833–1901)** became the twenty-third president of the United States in 1889. He was the grandson of William Henry Harrison (our country's ninth president) and a resident of Indianapolis. Before becoming president, he was commander of an Indiana volunteer-soldier troop in the Civil War, a lawyer, and a United States senator representing Indiana (1881–1887).

## TURN OF THE CENTURY

By the beginning of the 1900s, Indiana had created a place for itself within the United States. Rich mineral resources brought new businesses, and Indiana transportation routes were busy. Another Hoosier, Benjamin Harrison, served as president of the United States from 1889 to 1893.

During this time, most Hoosiers moved to the cities to work in factories. Standard Oil built its oil refinery in the northwestern Calumet region, as did the United States Steel Corporation. In 1905, U.S. Steel created an entire city around its plants. It was named Gary, after the head of the company. By 1920, the Calumet region was one of the leading centers of manufacturing and business in North America.

The early 1900s was a period of growth in the automobile industry in Indiana. Inventors and engineers all over the state created new types of cars. The Studebaker company in South Bend, which had begun making wagons and carriages in 1858, started producing cars. Other car factories opened in Elkhart, Auburn, and Indianapolis. So many cars were invented that car manufacturers built a racetrack called the Indianapolis Motor Speedway, where they could test and race new cars. It opened in 1909.

The new jobs attracted many people from southern and eastern Europe to Indiana. These Europeans brought special skills in glassmaking, furniture building, and brick and tile making. This increased the kinds of industry in the state. In 1920 Indiana had a population of almost 3 million people, many of whom lived in the cities.

The unique look of Studebaker cars made the company famous.

## EXTRA! EXTRA!

The Indianapolis Motor Speedway was once paved with bricks, earning it the nickname The Brickyard. It is one of the most famous venues for car races, including the annual Indianapolis 500 Auto Race, one of the biggest single-day sports events in the world. Race cars must make 200 laps around the track to complete this 500-mile (805-km) race. Another big event at the Speedway is the Brickyard 400. Every August, thousands of fans show up to watch this popular NASCAR race.

In 1917, America entered World War I (1914–1918). The United States joined the Allied countries (Great Britain, France, Belgium, Italy, Japan, Portugal, Romania, and Russia) to fight against Germany, Austria-Hungry, Bulgaria, and Turkey. Extra food was needed for the troops, as were steel and other products for military machinery. The increased demand helped both farmers and manufacturing businesses in Indiana. About 133,000 troops from Indiana fought in the war.

For several years after the war, most people in Indiana and the rest of the country enjoyed a good and prosperous life. However, people and businesses were doing so well that many had become careless with their money, spending too much and not saving enough to pay bills. Companies made more products than they could sell, and many had to close. Banks went out of business. This was the beginning of a difficult time in United States history known as the Great Depression (1929–1939).

This photo shows a view of Main Street in a rural town in Indiana during the 1920s.

The Great Depression affected people all over the country and the world. People throughout Indiana lost their jobs when companies closed down. One Hoosier said, "Everybody was having a hard time getting on. There was no money, not too many jobs, and the ones that had a job were very lucky to have it." The United States government provided help by setting up programs that offered jobs. One such program was the Works Progress Administration (WPA), which provided government money for new projects and offered jobs to workers, writers, and artists.

In January 1937, a terrible natural disaster added to Indiana's problems. After a long period of rain, the Ohio River overflowed and flooded much of southern Indiana. Hundreds of people died in the flood, acres of farmland were destroyed, and property damage was estimated at hundreds of millions of dollars.

Both Indiana's and the nation's economy finally started to recover after World War II (1939–1945) began. In 1941, the United States joined Great Britain, France, and Russia in the fight against Germany, Italy, and Japan. War goods were again needed, including guns, tanks, airplanes, and communications equipment. These were manufactured in Indiana's factories. Medicine for wounded soldiers was made in the state's drug companies.

Many women became factory workers during World War II, taking over for men who fought in the war.

Thousands of Hoosiers went back to work. When the men went off to war, Indiana women took over their jobs in the factories. More than 400,000 Indiana citizens fought or helped in the war effort.

## MAKING PROGRESS

After the war, farming became big business in Indiana. Large companies bought small farms and merged them together. Because the bigger companies used machines to do the work, farm production increased, but the number of farm workers grew smaller. As a result, many farmers moved to cities and took manufacturing jobs.

As the farm population decreased, the population in the cities grew. Large manufacturing cities, including Gary and Indianapolis, attracted workers, including African-Americans. However, although African-Americans had gained their rights after the Civil War, they were not treated well in many parts of the country, including Indiana.

"Jim Crow" laws were enforced in many states in an effort to segregate, or separate blacks and whites. These laws prevented African-Americans from using the same public facilities, such as drinking fountains or bathrooms, as whites. Many African-Americans had to attend separate schools. In 1927, a school called Crispus Attucks High School was built in Indianapolis just for African-American students.

Many African-Americans protested these unfair practices. In 1949, a law went into effect that made separate schooling for African-Americans and whites illegal. By the 1960s, more laws protecting the rights of African-Americans were passed.

African-Americans in Gary protested the unfair practice of school segregation.

## MODERN TIMES

The 1970s began on a good note, as a major seaport was built in Indiana. The Port of Indiana in Burns Harbor on Lake Michigan opened in 1970 to serve oceangoing ships. The port connects ships from around the world to Great Lakes ports by way of the St. Lawrence Seaway. It continues to be an international route for cargo ships.

By the late 1970s and early 1980s, the demand for steel, automobiles, and other manufactured goods had dropped. This caused companies to cut back on how much they produced. Many Hoosiers lost their jobs. Gary was one of the hardest-hit cities. Throughout the 1980s, companies closed or cut back their work force. Many people lost their jobs and left the city.

Founded as a grand industrial city, today Gary is being redeveloped and its history preserved.

In 1967, an African-American named Richard Hatcher became the mayor of Gary. He was one of the first African-American mayors of a major city. He served five terms, until 1987. During the difficult time in the 1980s, Hatcher helped provide employment and better housing for the people in Gary.

Indiana's economy improved in the 1990s. The state's farming businesses were again profitable. Indiana manufacturers began developing new businesses making electronic equipment such as video and DVD players, and high-technology products such as electrical switching devices, computers, and television sets.

As Indiana appoached the year 2000, two of its biggest challenges were to provide better education and a cleaner environment. The state spent more money on education and on programs to help the environment. For years, large steel and manufacturing operations in the cities around Lake Michigan had dumped waste products into the lake. As a result, many parts of the Indiana Harbor had become polluted. Today the harbor is being cleaned.

Indiana continues to be a major manufacturing state. Eli Lilly and Company is an international drug company with sales around the world.

Eli Lilly and Company, headquartered in Indianapolis, is a leader in the pharmaceutical industry.

Other Indiana manufacturers lead the nation in the production of medications and vitamins, surgical supplies, aircraft engines and parts, compact discs, musical instruments, truck and bus bodies, electronic resistors, and steel. Today these products are also sold to many foreign businesses.

Many cities, such as Indianapolis, have begun redevelopment projects. They are rebuilding and cleaning up older sections of the cities. Hoosiers continue to use inventiveness and imagination to find new ways to help their state grow and prosper.

# CHAPTER FOUR

# GOVERNING INDIANA

**I**ndiana's first constitution was created in 1816, the year Indiana became a state. A constitution is a system of laws that defines how a nation, a state, or a group is organized. Indiana's constitution states the rights of its citizens and also determines the powers of its government. The 1816 constitution had two special provisions or conditions that many other states did not have at the time: it prohibited (banned) slavery, and also called for the establishment of free, or public, schools. Indiana was the first state to declare that education should be available to everyone. In 1851 a new constitution was adopted and, although some changes have been made, it is still used today.

Indiana's government is made up of three parts, or branches: the executive branch, the legislative branch, and the judicial branch. These three groups work together to run the state.

The Indiana state capitol houses all three branches of the state government.

Indiana's state representatives meet in the house chambers inside the capitol building.

46

## EXECUTIVE BRANCH

The executive branch enforces, or carries out, the laws of the state. The governor is head of the executive branch. He or she is elected to a four-year term and may not serve more than two terms in a row. The governor has the power to appoint (select) and remove the people in charge of state government agencies, such as the department of natural resources and the bureau of motor vehicles.

Other people in the executive branch help the governor do his job. These officials include the lieutenant governor, the attorney general, the secretary of state, the treasurer, the auditor of state, the superintendent of public instruction, and the clerk of courts. All state officials in Indiana are elected to four-year terms.

## LEGISLATIVE BRANCH

The legislative branch creates laws to help the people of Indiana. For example, legislators (members of the legislative branch) might make laws that provide money to build public schools or to improve roads.

Legislators also make up the state's budget, a plan for how money will be spent to run all the services in the state.

Indiana's legislature is known as the General Assembly. It is made up of two parts, called houses: a house of representatives and a senate. The house of representatives has one hundred members. The senate has fifty members. Senators serve four-year terms, and representatives serve two-year terms. The General Assembly meets in January.

## JUDICIAL BRANCH

The judicial branch is made up of courts and judges, whose job is to interpret (explain) the laws and decide whether a law has been broken. The courts also determine the punishment for breaking a law. The judicial branch consists of the Indiana supreme court, the court of appeals, and ninety trial courts.

Trial courts are made up of local, county, circuit, and superior courts. All Indiana counties have circuit courts, and many also have county and superior courts. Circuit, superior, and county courts hear criminal trials. These may involve serious issues such as robbery, or misdemeanors (minor offenses) such as vandalism (the destruction of property). A few cities and towns have local courts that hear only minor cases, such as traffic violations or disputes involving money. Most county, circuit, and superior court judges are elected for six-year terms.

If a person is not satisfied with the court's decision, he or she may take their case to the court of appeals. An *appeal* is when someone asks a higher court to review a case and determine if the lower court's decision was fair. There are fifteen judges on the court of appeals.

The highest, or most important, court in Indiana is the state supreme court. The supreme court is the final place for appeals in the state of Indiana. It is currently made up of five justices (judges) chosen by the governor. A new justice serves for two years; then voters decide whether he or she may serve for ten more years. A special committee selects one of the justices to serve as chief justice for a five-year term.

Indiana also has a special court that many states do not have: a tax court. Tax court hears cases that involve disagreements over the payment of state taxes.

## TAXES IN INDIANA

As in other states, people in Indiana pay taxes. Taxes are required payments of money to the government. Tax money is used to pay for roads, schools, police and fire departments, the postal system, and public libraries, among other things.

Some taxes are based on income, which is the money a person earns or receives. These are called *income* taxes, and they are paid to the state government as well as to the United States government. *Sales* tax is paid upon purchase of certain items such as clothes, furniture, toys, or books. Other taxes include *property* taxes, which are paid on property such as a house, car, or boat; and *business* taxes. Businesses pay taxes on their profit, which is the amount of money left after all the costs of running the business have been subtracted from the money earned.

# INDIANA STATE GOVERNMENT

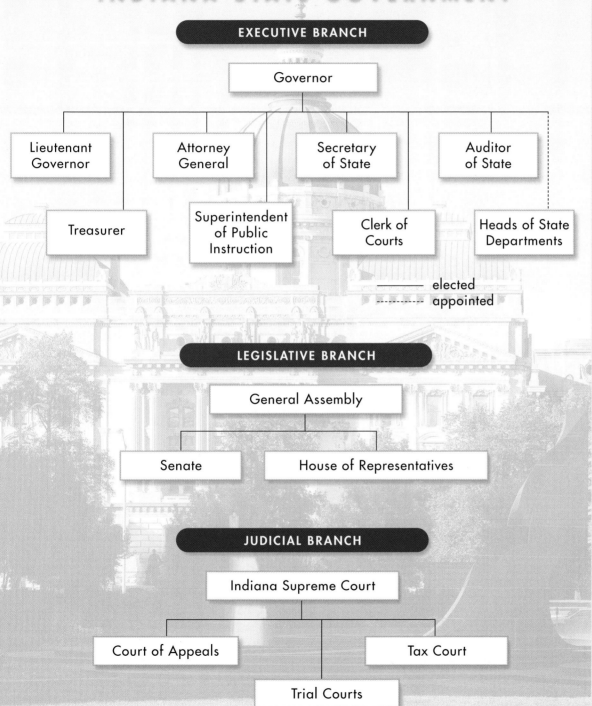

**EXECUTIVE BRANCH**

Governor

Lieutenant Governor

Attorney General

Secretary of State

Auditor of State

Treasurer

Superintendent of Public Instruction

Clerk of Courts

Heads of State Departments

——— elected

- - - - - appointed

**LEGISLATIVE BRANCH**

General Assembly

Senate

House of Representatives

**JUDICIAL BRANCH**

Indiana Supreme Court

Court of Appeals

Tax Court

Trial Courts

# INDIANA GOVERNORS

| Name | Term | Name | Term |
| --- | --- | --- | --- |
| Jonathon Jennings | 1816–1822 | Winfield T. Durbin | 1901–1905 |
| Ratliff Boon | 1822 | J. Frank Hanly | 1905–1909 |
| William Hendricks | 1822–1825 | Thomas R. Marshall | 1909–1913 |
| James B. Ray | 1825–1831 | Samuel M. Ralston | 1913–1917 |
| Noah Noble | 1831–1837 | James P. Goodrich | 1917–1921 |
| David Wallace | 1837–1840 | Warren T. McCray | 1921–1924 |
| Samuel Bigger | 1840–1843 | Emmett Forest Branch | 1924–1925 |
| James Whitcom | 1843–1848 | Ed Jackson | 1925–1929 |
| Paris C. Dunning | 1848–1849 | Harry G. Leslie | 1929–1933 |
| Joseph A. Wright | 1849–1857 | Paul V. McNutt | 1933–1937 |
| Ashbel P. Willard | 1857–1860 | M. Clifford Townsend | 1937–1941 |
| Abraham A. Hammond | 1860–1861 | Henry F. Schricker | 1941–1945 |
| Henry Smith Lane | 1861 | Ralph F. Gates | 1945–1949 |
| Oliver P. Morton | 1861–1867 | Henry F. Schricker | 1949–1953 |
| Conrad Baker | 1867–1873 | George N. Craig | 1953–1957 |
| Thomas A. Hendricks | 1873–1877 | Harold W. Handley | 1957–1961 |
| James D. Williams | 1877–1880 | Matthew E. Welsh | 1961–1965 |
| Isaac P. Gray | 1880–1881 | Roger D. Branigin | 1965–1969 |
| Albert G. Porter | 1881–1885 | Edgar D. Whitcomb | 1969–1973 |
| Isaac P. Gray | 1885–1889 | Otis R. Bowen | 1973–1981 |
| Alvin P. Hovey | 1889–1891 | Robert D. Orr | 1981–1989 |
| Ira Joy Chase | 1891–1893 | Evan Bayh | 1989–1997 |
| Claude Matthews | 1893–1897 | Frank O'Bannon | 1997– |
| James A. Mount | 1897–1901 | | |

Indianapolis is located in the center of the state on the White River. The city was founded in 1820 and settled by a mix of people including Germans, Irish, African-Americans, Italians, and Eastern Europeans. German-American architects designed many of the city's churches, public buildings, and monuments. Indianapolis became Indiana's third capital in 1825.

The highlight of the downtown area is the capitol building, an impressive structure that was built using materials from Indiana, including Indiana oak, maple, and walnut woods, and limestone. Inside there are beautiful marble columns, floors, and statues. The capitol has a central dome made of copper and a rotunda (a large circular room) with an art glass inner dome hanging below a skylight. The governor and other members of the executive branch work inside the capitol, as does the Indiana General Assembly, the state supreme court, and the court of appeals.

Not far from the capitol is Monument Circle. This circle has the 284-foot- (87-m-) high Soldiers and Sailors Monument at its

As the nation's 12th largest city, Indianapolis is rich in arts, culture, and history.

## FIND OUT MORE

In 1878, when construction began on the capitol building, a cornerstone of Indiana limestone was laid. Hidden inside the cornerstone are forty-two items from the 1800s. They include government reports; a Bible; forty-seven kinds of Indiana-grown cereal and vegetable seeds sealed in small glass cases; new coins; maps; newspapers; pamphlets; and a history of the city. If you could create a time capsule for today, what would you include?

The Soldiers and Sailors Monument is dedicated to Indiana's war heroes.

center. It is topped by a statue of Victory, known as Miss Indiana. If you climb up to the observation deck, you'll see a fantastic view of the city. The city streets spread out in a wheel pattern from Monument Circle.

At the base of the monument is the Colonel Eli Lilly Museum. Inside you'll find exhibits about Indiana during the Civil War. You can see pictures of Indiana soldiers and read accounts of the battles.

The history of the state is well documented. The Indiana State Museum and the Indiana Historical Society have exhibits that tell the history of Indiana since the pioneer era. Inside the Indiana State Museum is Freetown Village, a "living history" museum that shows how African-Americans lived in the 1870s. More African-American history can be found at the Madame Walker Theatre Building, a National Historic Landmark. It was built in the 1920s to show the historic achievements and contributions of Madame C. J. Walker. Today it is a cultural center for the African-American community.

Other interesting museums include the Indiana Medical History Museum, which houses almost 15,000 medical instruments used throughout history. The Indianapolis Museum of Art, one of the oldest art museums in the United States, has a great art collection. The

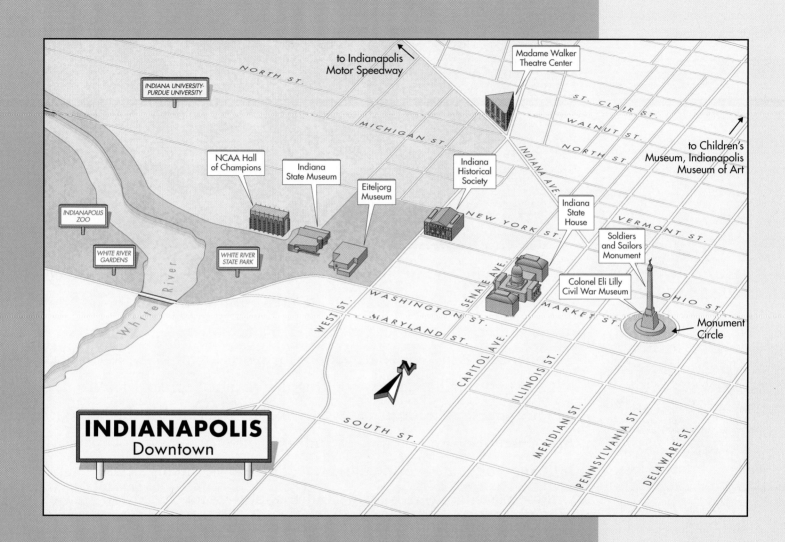

to Indianapolis
Motor Speedway

Madame Walker
Theatre Center

to Children's
Museum, Indianapolis
Museum of Art

INDIANA UNIVERSITY-
PURDUE UNIVERSITY

NCAA Hall
of Champions

Indiana
State Museum

Eiteljorg
Museum

Indiana
Historical
Society

Indiana
State
House

INDIANAPOLIS
ZOO

Soldiers
and Sailors
Monument

WHITE RIVER
GARDENS

WHITE RIVER
STATE PARK

Colonel Eli Lilly
Civil War Museum

Monument
Circle

**INDIANAPOLIS**
Downtown

NORTH ST.

MICHIGAN ST.

ST. CLAIR ST.

WALNUT ST.

NORTH ST.

INDIANA AVE.

NEW YORK ST.

VERMONT ST.

OHIO ST.

SENATE AVE.

WASHINGTON ST.

MARKET ST.

CAPITOL AVE.

MARYLAND ST.

ILLINOIS ST.

MERIDIAN ST.

PENNSYLVANIA ST.

DELAWARE ST.

WEST ST.

SOUTH ST.

White River

N

A racing crew gathers around a racecar at the Indianapolis Motor Speedway.

Children's Museum of Indianapolis is one of the world's largest children's museums. There you can ride on a turn-of-the-century carousel or sail through space in the SpaceQuest Planetarium.

Indianapolis has lots of attractions for sports lovers. The NCAA Hall of Champions has a video wall of highlights in college sports. Also, the nation's largest collection of sport-related art is located at the National Art Museum on the campus of Indiana University–Purdue University Indianapolis. The world's largest collection of racing, classic, and antique passenger cars is at the Indianapolis Motor Speedway Hall of Fame Museum, right next to the world-famous speedway.

At the edge of downtown Indianapolis is White River State Park. This park contains the Indianapolis Zoo, the White River Botanical Gardens, and the Eiteljorg Museum of American Indians and Western Art. It is the only museum in the Midwest to combine Western art and Native American art.

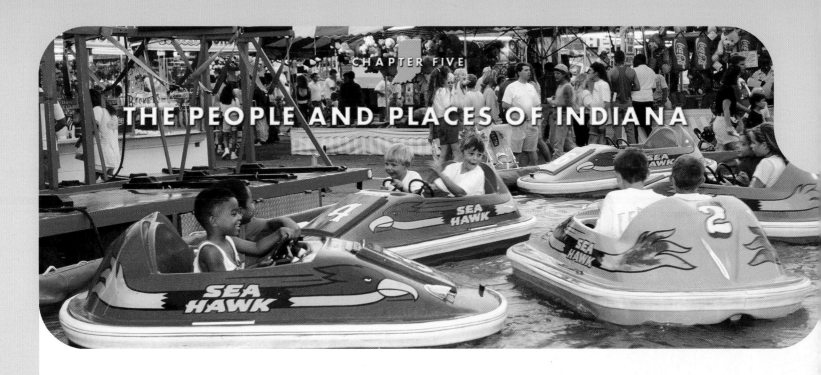

# CHAPTER FIVE

# THE PEOPLE AND PLACES OF INDIANA

**I**ndiana is a small state with a large population. Among the states, it ranks 38th in size and 14th in population, with more than 6 million people. Almost 7 in every 10 people live in the cities. The largest city is Indianapolis, followed by Fort Wayne, Evansville, and South Bend.

Almost 9 in every 10 people are of European descent. Indiana was first settled by people from France and England. Later, immigrants from Germany, Scotland, Ireland, and Eastern European countries arrived. Many Polish, Hungarian, Belgian, and Italian groups can also be found in cities throughout the northern part of the state.

While the numbers of other ethnic groups are growing, they are still small. About 8 in every 100 people are African-American, and 5 in every 100 people are either Hispanic, Native American, or Asian. Most of these ethnic groups are found in the larger cities.

Young Hoosiers enjoy the rides at the Indiana State Fair in Indianapolis.

55

Fewer than 14,000 Native Americans live in Indiana. The Miami and the Potawatomi are the largest Native American groups. Throughout the 1900s, members of both tribes moved back to Indiana from Kansas and Oklahoma. They are located mainly in Miami, Wabash, Grant, Allen, Howard, and Huntington counties.

A scientist at Lilly Pharmaceuticals in Indianapolis works in a drug research laboratory.

## WORKING IN INDIANA

Indiana is one of the leading manufacturing states. It ranks as one of the top five states for producing items such as surgical supplies, aircraft engines and parts, medical drug products, compact discs, musical instruments, truck and bus bodies, electronic resistors, and steel. Trucks, car parts, and aircraft engines are made in Indianapolis and shipped to all parts of the United States and overseas. Chemicals, electrical equipment, and machinery are also produced in Indianapolis. Flour milling, meatpacking, vegetable processing, and printing are other industries in the city. Indianapolis is also one of the main transportation centers in the Midwest.

Fort Wayne is known for the manufacture of a wide variety of machinery, electronics, and metal goods. The city produces a large amount of the world's supply of diamond tools, used for making jewelry. Gary and Hammond produce iron, steel, and oil products. Elkhart manufactures medical drugs and is known worldwide for its excellent production of musical instruments. In South Bend, farm machinery, surgical supplies, tools and dies, aircraft equipment, clothing, and transportation equipment are manufactured.

One of the largest areas of employment in Indiana is the service industry. This industry includes jobs that provide a service, such as waiters and waitresses, bank tellers, store clerks, health care workers, real estate agents, and school teachers. Many people in the service industry work at health care companies.

The tourism industry is growing in the state. Most tourists visit the northern lakes, the southern shore of Lake Michigan, and the forests of southern Indiana. The Indianapolis 500 race and other major sports events also attract tourists.

Indiana is the 15th largest farming state in the nation. Most of the state's farming industry is concentrated in central Indiana. Indiana is a top producer of corn and soybeans. Wheat, oats, hay, rye, tomatoes, cucumbers, potatoes, apples, and peaches are other important crops. Indiana is also among the nation's leading producers of spearmint and peppermint, both of which are grown in the wet soils of the northern lake region.

Hogs and cattle are the state's major livestock products. Farmers also raise dairy cattle, turkeys, ducks, chickens, sheep, and horses. The principal dairy products in Indiana are milk and eggs. California is the only state that produces more eggs than Indiana.

## EXTRA! EXTRA!

Gourmet popcorn was born in Valparaiso, Indiana, a small town in northwestern Indiana. The popcorn was developed there in the 1950s by a local farmer named Orville Redenbacher. Today, more than 254 million pounds of popcorn are grown on Indiana land, mostly around Valparaiso.

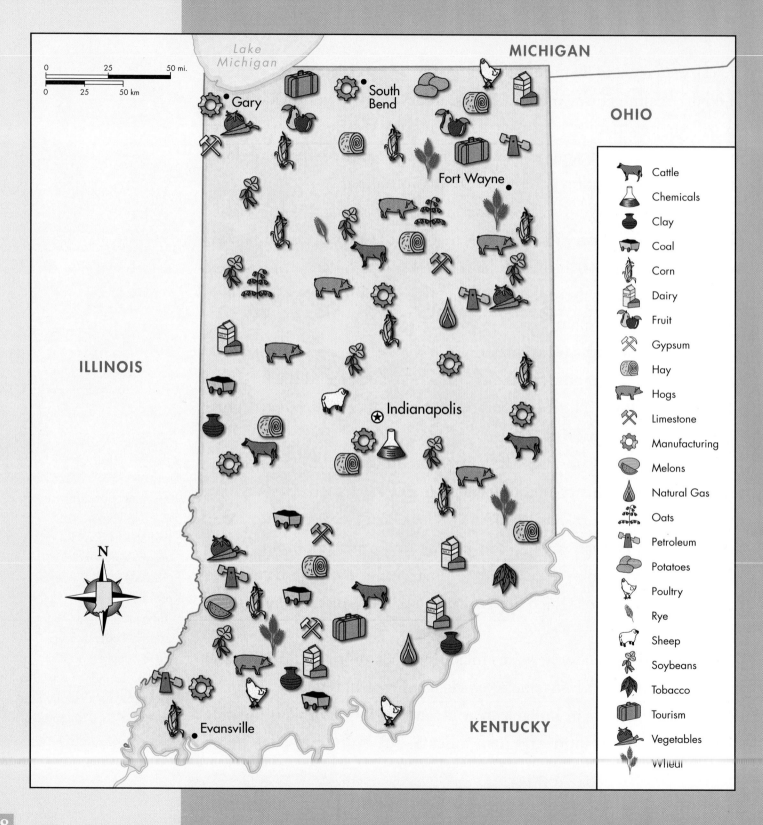

Lake Michigan

MICHIGAN

OHIO

ILLINOIS

Gary

South Bend

Fort Wayne

Indianapolis

Evansville

KENTUCKY

0    25    50 mi.

0    25    50 km

N

| | |
|---|---|
| 🐄 | Cattle |
| ⚗ | Chemicals |
| 🏺 | Clay |
| | Coal |
| 🌽 | Corn |
| 🥛 | Dairy |
| 🍎 | Fruit |
| ⚒ | Gypsum |
| | Hay |
| 🐖 | Hogs |
| ⚒ | Limestone |
| ⚙ | Manufacturing |
| | Melons |
| 💧 | Natural Gas |
| | Oats |
| | Petroleum |
| | Potatoes |
| 🐓 | Poultry |
| | Rye |
| 🐑 | Sheep |
| 🌿 | Soybeans |
| | Tobacco |
| 🧳 | Tourism |
| | Vegetables |
| | Wheat |

58

The Hoosier State is a leading producer of soybeans. Tofu is made from soybeans and is great for mixing with other foods. Make this yummy salad recipe and you'll have a tasty, healthy Indiana soybean dish.

### FRUITY SALAD WITH TOFU AND HONEY DRESSING
(makes about 8 servings)

Salad:
   1/4 cup fresh lemon juice
   1 cup water
   4 large apples, sliced
   1/2 cup golden raisins
   1 orange, cut into small pieces
   1 8-ounce can pineapple tidbits, drained
   3 stalks celery, sliced
   1/3 cup chopped walnuts or pecans
   6 lettuce leaves torn in smaller pieces

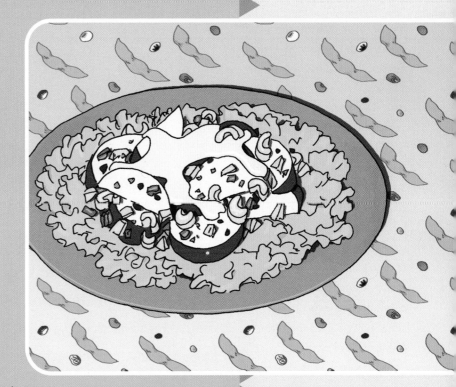

Dressing:
   1/2 cup soft silken tofu
   1 cup plain or pineapple yogurt
   3 tablespoons honey
   1 teaspoon ground cinnamon

1. Make the dressing first. Mash the tofu with a fork. Combine the mashed tofu with yogurt, honey, and cinnamon.
2. Beat the mixture with a spoon. Stir until smooth. (If needed, add a small amount of water to make it smoother.) Put dressing in refrigerator to chill.
3. Mix lemon juice and water, then add sliced apples and toss. (This keeps the cut apples from turning brown.) Drain apples, pouring off the liquid.
4. Combine apples, raisins, orange, pineapple, celery, and nuts.
5. Put fruit mixture on the lettuce leaves. Pour tofu dressing on top, and enjoy!

Almost 2.1 million pounds of Indiana limestone was used to replace sections of the Pentagon in Washington, D.C., that were damaged or destroyed by the terrorist attack of September 11, 2001. More than 4,000 new limestone blocks were cut and shaped for the building. This piece of Indiana limestone (shown right) contains a quote from President George W. Bush and the signatures of Indiana stonecutters, Washington D.C. construction workers, and New York police officers and firefighters. The stone will be preserved for a future display at the Pentagon or a museum.

Coal mining takes place in southwestern Indiana. Limestone is quarried in the south central region. Indiana is the major source for limestone used in the building industry. Indiana limestone has been used for many famous structures such as the Empire State Building and the Pentagon. Clay, gravel, stone, oil, and gypsum are also mined.

## TAKE A TOUR OF INDIANA

### Northwest Indiana

Let's begin our tour in the northwestern corner of the state at the southern tip of Lake Michigan. The Indiana Dunes State Park and Indiana Dunes National Lakeshore offer 22 miles (35 km) of white sand dunes and beaches. A nature center offers details of the history of the dunes area. Nearby Michigan City has the state's only working lighthouse and the Old Lighthouse Museum.

Also on Lake Michigan is Gary, the fifth largest city in the state. It is the home of the steel industry in America, as well as the birthplace of pop star Michael Jackson. The northern region of Indiana has a number of lakes and state parks that provide more places for outdoor fun.

In northwest Indiana, you'll find some great car museums. The Door Prairie Auto Museum in La Porte has more than 50 historical vehicles and an example of the world's first car. The Studebaker Museum in South Bend shows a collection of old cars, carriages, and wagons.

This photograph shows a young Amish girl near Shipshewana.

Also in South Bend is the College Football Hall of Fame and the University of Notre Dame, home of the Fighting Irish football team. The University of Notre Dame opened in 1842 and is considered one of the best Roman Catholic universities in the United States. Originally a school for men, Notre Dame now enrolls women from nearby St. Mary's College.

East of South Bend you'll find Amish country in the region around Elkhart, Nappanee, and Shipshewana. The Amish are a religious group whose beliefs prevent them from using modern technology such as electricity and automobiles. They live in rural farming communities and lead a simple life. At Amish Acres in Nappanee you can see how the Amish live and work.

**Gene Stratton-Porter
(1863–1924)** was best
known for her popular
novels *Freckles, A Girl of the
Limberlost, Laddie,* and *A
Daughter of the Land,* some
of which were made into
movies. She also gained
fame for her photographs
of birds and animals.

Northeast Indiana

In the northeastern part of the state you'll find Rome City and the Gene Stratton-Porter Home, a state historic site. This 16-room cabin was home to Gene Stratton-Porter, an Indiana author and photographer. Farther south is Limberlost State Historic Site, another home of Stratton-Porter. It was named for nearby Limberlost Swamp. Don't miss seeing the fascinating moth collection there!

Fort Wayne offers a rebuilt version of the historic fort, and the Lincoln Museum has interesting multimedia exhibits that tell the story of Abraham Lincoln and his boyhood spent in Indiana. If you like animals, the Fort Wayne Children's Zoo is a fun place to visit. You can get a close-up view of penguins, giraffes, tigers, and other animals at the zoo, or hop on board the zoo train and get a look around the park.

Zookeepers feed the penguins at the Fort Wayne Children's Zoo.

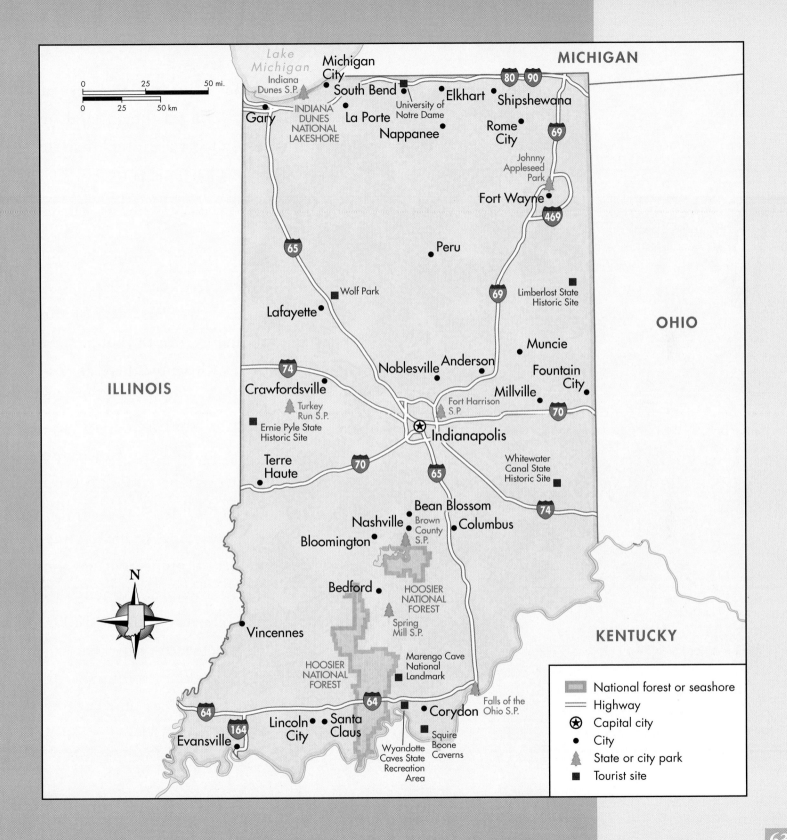

Lake
Michigan

MICHIGAN

Michigan
City

Indiana
Dunes S.P.

South Bend

Gary

INDIANA
DUNES
NATIONAL
LAKESHORE

La Porte

Elkhart

University of
Notre Dame

Nappanee

Shipshewana

Rome
City

80 90

69

Johnny
Appleseed
Park

Fort Wayne

469

65

Peru

Wolf Park

69

Limberlost State
Historic Site

OHIO

Lafayette

Muncie

74

Noblesville

Anderson

Fountain
City

Crawfordsville

Millville

Fort Harrison
S.P.

70

ILLINOIS

Turkey
Run S.P.

Indianapolis

Ernie Pyle State
Historic Site

Whitewater
Canal State
Historic Site

Terre
Haute

70

65

74

Bean Blossom

Nashville

Brown
County
S.P.

Columbus

Bloomington

Bedford

HOOSIER
NATIONAL
FOREST

Spring
Mill S.P.

N

Vincennes

Marengo Cave
National
Landmark

KENTUCKY

HOOSIER
NATIONAL
FOREST

64

Lincoln
City

Santa
Claus

64

164

Evansville

Corydon

Falls of the
Ohio S.P.

Squire
Boone
Caverns

Wyandotte
Caves State
Recreation
Area

0   25   50 mi.

0   25   50 km

National forest or seashore

Highway

Capital city

City

State or city park

Tourist site

63

Johnny Appleseed Park offers another kind of history—the story of Johnny Appleseed. Johnny's real name was John Chapman, and he became famous when he wandered through Indiana planting his apple trees. Books and songs have been written about his Indiana travels.

### WHO'S WHO IN INDIANA?

**Wilbur Wright (1867– 1912)** was one of the most famous inventors in airplane history. Born in Millville, Wilbur and his brother Orville invented and flew the first practical airplane, then made the first powered airplane flights in history. He also set distance and altitude (height) records.

## Central Indiana

You'll find the cities of Anderson and Muncie in central Indiana. Anderson is home to Mounds State Park, one of the sites of Native American earth mounds. At Muncie Children's Museum, there are exhibits featuring the cartoon cat Garfield. The cartoon's creator, Jim Davis, is an Indiana native and lives in the area. Muncie also offers the Wilbur Wright Museum with some great airplane exhibits.

In Fishers, history comes to life at Conner Prairie, a re-created pioneer village and museum. In Prairietown, costumed staff members act like pioneers from the 1800s. Visitors can try nineteenth-century activities such as candle making, spinning, and weaving. You can also see a recreated Lenape Indian camp from 1816.

## Southern Indiana

The south central region is home to the beautiful Hoosier National Forest. There are many things to see and do there, both indoors and outdoors.

At Spring Mill State Park you can take a boat ride into Twin Caves or walk through Donaldson Cave. At the entrance to the park is a 30-foot (9-m) limestone statue of a rocket. This is a memorial to famous astronaut Virgil "Gus" Grissom, who captained the *Mercury* and *Gemini* space flights before dying in the *Apollo 1* disaster. Inside the memorial are exhibits about Grissom's career as a test pilot and in the space program.

Nearby Nashville and Bloomington offer lots of art, history, and other interesting things. Bloomington is the site of the main campus of Indiana University. Visit the university's excellent art museum and see the many art galleries in town. The Bloomington Speedway draws dirt-track and midget-car racing fans.

Hoosier National Forest is a great place for hiking, camping, horseback riding, and more.

## WHO'S WHO IN INDIANA?

**Hoagy Carmichael (1899–1981)** was a musician and songwriter who composed many well-known songs. In 1971 he was one of the first ten artists elected to the Songwriters Hall of Fame. Carmichael was born in Bloomington.

The Ameritech building in Columbus is one example of the city's unusual architecture.

Columbus is called the Architectural Showplace of America. Many of the city's buildings were designed by famous 20th-century architects. The Columbus Visitor Center has displays highlighting the city's architectural history.

Close to Columbus is a small town with the interesting name of Bean Blossom. It is a great place to hear bluegrass and other types of country music. The Bill Monroe Museum and Bluegrass Hall of Fame has information about the history of bluegrass music and holds a big music festival every summer.

Historic Corydon was Indiana's first state capital. At the Corydon Capital Historic Site you can tour the old capitol building and the governor's house. During the summer, visitors can ride the Corydon Scenic Railroad through the surrounding countryside.

Next door is Lincoln City, and the Lincoln Boyhood National Memorial. It contains the 16th president's childhood home and his mother's grave, as well as a re-created pioneer farm of the 1820s.

Located at the southeast tip of Indiana is Evansville, home to the University of Southern Indiana, the University of Evansville, and the Evansville Museum of Arts and Sciences. Just outside the city is the Angel Mounds State Memorial Park.

Costumed guides demonstrate daily chores and frontier farming methods at the Lincoln Living Historical Farm.

## Western Indiana

Western Indiana is nationally known for its 32 covered bridges and its beautiful scenery. In the fall, the roads are crowded with people taking pictures of the colorful trees.

Vincennes was Indiana's first European settlement and the first capital of the Indiana Territory. It is located along the Wabash River and offers many historic sites. You can tour the Indiana Territory's capitol building, George Rogers Clark National Historical Park, and the restored home of a French fur trader from the 1700s.

The George Rogers Clark National Memorial commemorates Lieutenant Colonel Clark's victory over the British at this site during the American Revolution.

Going north you'll arrive at Terre Haute, the birthplace of Paul Dresser, who wrote Indiana's state song, "On the Banks of the Wabash, Far Away." You can see his home and then tour the Fowler Park Pioneer Settlement to see pioneer history.

Just above Terre Haute is the Indiana Parke County area, also known as "covered bridge country." Located around the town of Billie Creek Village are three covered bridges: Leatherwood Station, Beeson, and Billie Creek. The town itself is a living-history museum that re-creates an early 1900s Indiana town.

Also in the area is the Ernie Pyle State Historic Site. A visit there will help you learn about the life and work of the world-renowned Pulitzer Prize-winning writer. You can also discover what life was like for an American soldier in World War II.

Our last stop is Crawfordsville, home of the General Lew Wallace Study and Ben-Hur Museum. Lew Wallace was the author of *Ben Hur*, a popular novel that later became a movie classic. The study is a grand structure that features items from Wallace's life and career. It was declared a National Historic Landmark in 1977.

The charm of Indiana lies in its mix of things to see and do. It is a combination of quiet towns, exciting sports events, unique museums, and fun outdoor activities.

# INDIANA ALMANAC

**Statehood date and number:** December 11, 1816/19th

**State seal:** Adopted in 1963. The state seal shows a pioneer scene. The sun setting behind the hills represents Indiana's historic position as a foothold in the west-ward movement.

**State flag:** Adopted in 1917. The flag has a torch in the center that represents ideas of liberty and enlighten-ment. The torch is surrounded by nineteen stars. The largest star represents Indiana.

**Geographic center:** Boone, 14 miles (23 km) N-NW of Indianapolis

**Total area/rank:** 36,420 square miles (94,327 sq km)/38th

**Borders:** Illinois, Michigan, Lake Michigan, Ohio, and Kentucky

**Latitude and longitude:** Indiana is located approxi-mately between 37° 47' and 41° 46' N and 84° 49' and 88° 02' W.

**Highest/lowest elevation:** Hoosier Hill, Wayne County; 1,257 feet (383 m)/Ohio River, Posey County; 320 feet (98 m)

**Hottest/coldest temperature:** 116° F (47° C) at Collegeville on July 14, 1936/–36° F (–38° C) at New Whiteland on January 19, 1994

**Land area/rank:** 35,870 square miles (92,903 sq km)/38th

**Inland water area:** 315 square miles (816 sq km)

**Population (2000 census)/rank:** 6,080,485/14th

**Population of major cities:**

Indianapolis: 791,926

**Fort Wayne:** 205,727

**Evansville:** 121,582

**South Bend:** 107,789

**Gary:** 102,746

**Hammond:** 83,048

**Origin of state name:** Means "Land of the Indians"

**State capital:** Indianapolis

**Previous capitals:** Vincennes (1800–1813) and Corydon (1813–1824)

**Counties:** 92

**State government:** 50 senators, 100 representatives

**Major lakes and rivers:** Lake Michigan, Lake Wawasee, Lake Mississinewa, Lake Monroe, Ohio River, Kankakee River, Wabash River, White River, Tippecanoe River

**Farm products:** Corn, soybeans, hogs, wheat, oats, hay, rye, tomatoes, cucumbers, potatoes, apples, peaches, spearmint, peppermint

**Livestock:** Hogs, cattle, poultry, sheep

**Manufactured products:** Transportation equipment, primary metals, chemicals, medical drugs, machinery, electrical equipment

**Mining products:** Coal, oil, natural gas, limestone, clay, gravel, stone, gypsum

**Bird:** Cardinal

**Flower:** Peony

**Motto:** Crossroads of America

**Nickname:** The Hoosier State

**Poem:** "Indiana," by Arthur Franklin Mapes

**Soil:** Miami soil

**Song:** "On the Banks of the Wabash, Far Away" by Paul Dresser

**Stone:** Salem limestone

**Tree:** Tulip tree

**Wildlife:** White-tailed deer, muskrats, coyotes, wild turkeys, striped gophers, woodchucks, red foxes, skunks, raccoons, mink, chipmunks, opossums, gray squirrels, beavers, cottontail rabbits

# TIME**LINE**

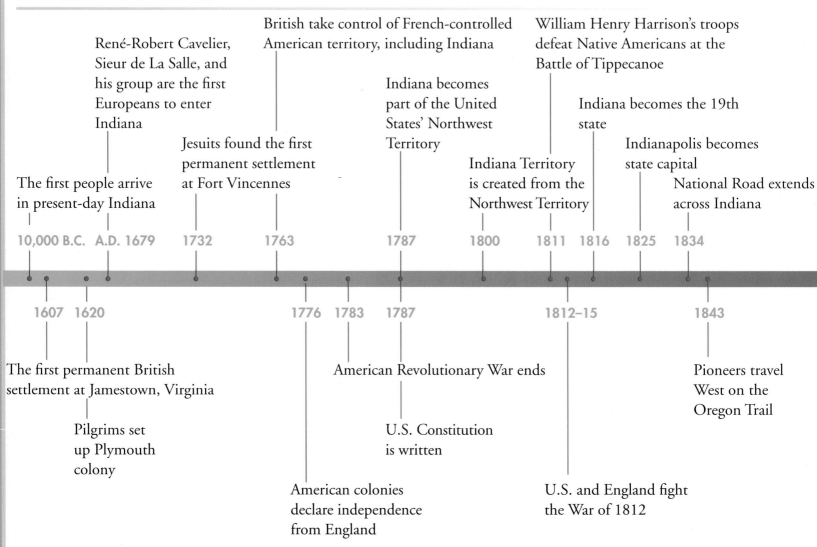

René-Robert Cavelier, Sieur de La Salle, and his group are the first Europeans to enter Indiana

British take control of French-controlled American territory, including Indiana

William Henry Harrison's troops defeat Native Americans at the Battle of Tippecanoe

Indiana becomes part of the United States' Northwest Territory

Indiana becomes the 19th state

Jesuits found the first permanent settlement at Fort Vincennes

Indianapolis becomes state capital

The first people arrive in present-day Indiana

Indiana Territory is created from the Northwest Territory

National Road extends across Indiana

10,000 B.C.   A.D. 1679   1732   1763   1787   1800   1811   1816   1825   1834

1607   1620   1776   1783   1787   1812–15   1843

The first permanent British settlement at Jamestown, Virginia

American Revolutionary War ends

Pioneers travel West on the Oregon Trail

Pilgrims set up Plymouth colony

U.S. Constitution is written

American colonies declare independence from England

U.S. and England fight the War of 1812

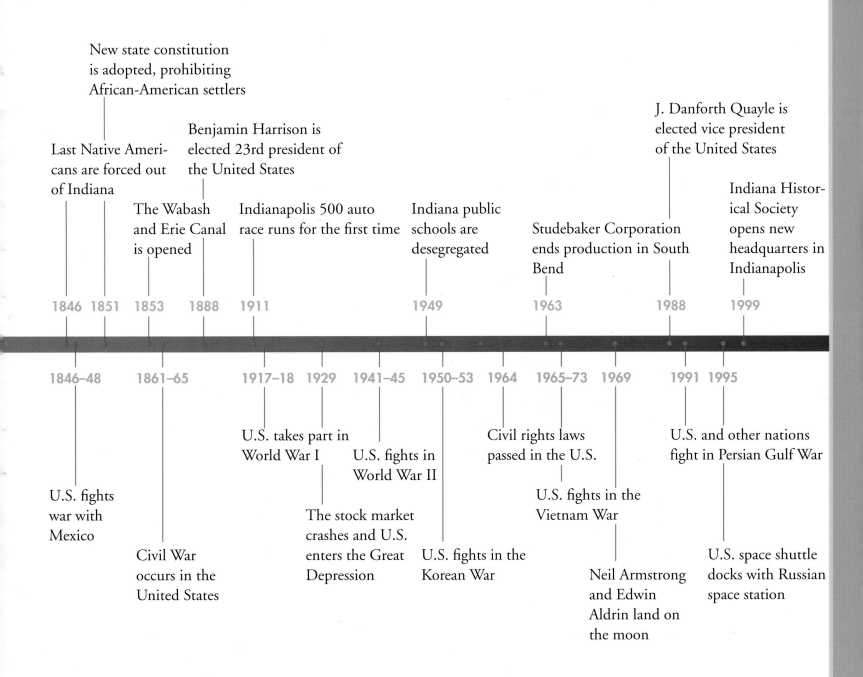

New state constitution is adopted, prohibiting African-American settlers

Last Native Americans are forced out of Indiana

Benjamin Harrison is elected 23rd president of the United States

J. Danforth Quayle is elected vice president of the United States

The Wabash and Erie Canal is opened

Indianapolis 500 auto race runs for the first time

Indiana public schools are desegregated

Studebaker Corporation ends production in South Bend

Indiana Historical Society opens new headquarters in Indianapolis

1846  1851  1853  1888  1911  1949  1963  1988  1999

1846–48  1861–65  1917–18  1929  1941–45  1950–53  1964  1965–73  1969  1991  1995

U.S. takes part in World War I

U.S. fights in World War II

Civil rights laws passed in the U.S.

U.S. and other nations fight in Persian Gulf War

U.S. fights war with Mexico

U.S. fights in the Vietnam War

The stock market crashes and U.S. enters the Great Depression

Civil War occurs in the United States

U.S. fights in the Korean War

Neil Armstrong and Edwin Aldrin land on the moon

U.S. space shuttle docks with Russian space station

# GALLERY OF FAMOUS HOOSIERS

## Larry Bird
(1956– )
Championship NBA player and coach of the Indiana Pacers. He was elected to the Basketball Hall of Fame in 1997. Born in West Baden.

## David Letterman
(1947– )
Comedian and talk show host of the late-night network television show *The Late Show with David Letterman*. Born in Indianapolis.

## Jane Pauley
(1950– )
American television broadcaster and reporter for *Dateline NBC*. She hosted NBC's *Today Show* from 1976 to 1990 and worked as a newscaster on NBC's *News Update* and *The NBC Nightly News*. Born in Indianapolis.

## Cole Porter
(1891–1964)
Famous American composer and songwriter. He wrote many famous songs for recordings and musical shows. Born in Peru.

## Frances Slocum
(1773–1847)
Quaker woman who was kidnapped by Delaware Native Americans when she was five years old. She was later raised by a Miami Native American couple near present-day Peru. Slocum gained fame as the White Rose of the Miamis, because she worked to bring peace between Native Americans and white settlers.

## Booth Tarkington
(1869–1946)
Novelist and playwright who received the Pulitzer Prize for novels *The Magnificent Ambersons* and *Alice Adams*. Born in Indianapolis.

## Twyla Tharp
(1941– )
Dancer and choreographer. She formed her own dance company, where she created a dance style that combined classical ballet with body movements from American tap, jazz, and social dance. Born in Portland.

## Kurt Vonnegut Jr.
(1922– )
Novelist who combined science fiction and social satire in his books. In 1999, he was honored by the Indiana Historical Society as an Indiana Living Legend. Born in Indianapolis.

# GLOSSARY

**aqueduct:** a large bridge built to carry water across a valley

**artifacts:** objects remaining from the past that were made by human beings, such as tools

**choreographer:** someone who arranges dance steps and movements for musicals and movies

**constitution:** a document that outlines the laws or principles by which a nation, a government, or a group is organized

**economy:** the careful use or management of resources, such as money, materials, or labor

**ethnicity:** a common racial, national, religious, or cultural heritage that is shared by a group of people

**fossil:** the remains or traces of an animal or plant from millions of years ago

**mammoth:** a large hairy extinct elephant that had long upward-curving teeth called tusks

**prehistoric:** belonging to or existing in a time before written history

**primitive:** the earliest or first stage of development; very simple

**refinery:** a factory where raw materials such as oil or metal are purified and made into finished products

**revolution:** a rebellion by the people of a country against their government to change the system under which they have been ruled; a complete change

**treaty:** a formal agreement outlining terms of peace or trade

# FOR MORE INFORMATION

## Web sites

**Indiana Historical Society**

*www.indianahistory.org/*

Collections of Indiana history documents. Information about the history of the state.

**Indiana State Library**

*http://www.statelib.lib.in.us/*

Documents on Indiana history and links to history resources.

**State of Indiana Website**

*http://www.IN.gov/*

The official web site of the state of Indiana.

**Visit Indiana**

*http://www.visitindiana.net/*

Information about Indiana historical sites, parks, nature areas, and unusual places to visit.

## Books

Chambers, Catherine E. *Indiana Days: Life in a Frontier Town* (Adventures in Frontier America). Mahwah, NJ: Troll Associates, 1999.

Hinshaw, Dorothy. *When I Was Young in Indiana: A Hoosier Life.* Zionsville, IN: Guild Press of Indiana, 1994.

Hiscock, Bruce. *The Big Rivers: The Missouri, the Mississippi, and the Ohio.* New York, NY: Atheneum, 1997.

McKenna, A. T. *Indy Racing* (Fast Tracks). Edina, MN: Abdo & Daughters, 1998.

Price, Nelson. *Legendary Hoosiers: Famous Folks from the State of Indiana.* Zionsville, IN: Guild Press of Indiana, 2001.

## Addresses

**Indiana Historical Society**

450 West Ohio Street
Indianapolis, IN 46202

**Indiana Historical Bureau**

140 North Senate Avenue, Room 408
Indianapolis, IN 46204

**Indiana State Information Center**

A Division of the Indiana Department of Administration
402 West Washington Street, Room W160A
Indianapolis, IN 46204

**Angel Mounds State Historic Site**

8215 Pollack Avenue
Evansville, IN 47715

# INDEX

## ABOUT THE AUTHOR

**Bettina Ling** has been a writer and an editor of educational material for sixteen years. She has written more than fourteen books for children and young adults, including *Wisconsin* in the From Sea to Shining Sea series. Some of her other titles are *Aung San Suu Kyi: Standing Up For Democracy In Burma*, *The Little Mermaid: Flounder to the Rescue*, and *The Fattest, Tallest, Biggest Snowman*. This book is dedicated to her parents, who met when they were students at Notre Dame University and St. Mary's College.